Jim Henson:
A Short Biography

EXPLORING THE THE LIFE AND WORK OF AN ENTERTAINMENT INNOVATOR

WILL ANDREWS

Copyright © 2023 Will Andrews

Table of Contents

Introduction: Setting the Stage

In the realm of creativity, there exist luminaries whose work transcends time, touching the hearts and minds of generations. One such visionary was Jim Henson, a creative genius whose imagination knew no bounds. Through the magic of puppetry, innovation, and boundless enthusiasm, Henson revolutionized the world of entertainment and left an indelible mark on the fabric of popular culture.

This meticulously detailed biography invites you to journey through the life and achievements of this remarkable artist. From his humble beginnings to his meteoric rise to fame, we will delve into the intricate tapestry of Henson's existence, weaving together his personal experiences, creative breakthroughs, and the profound impact he made on the world.

Setting the Stage: The Birth of a Creative Genius

We begin by exploring the backdrop against which Jim Henson's life unfolded. From his family background and early influences to the nurturing of his artistic talents, this section lays the foundation for the remarkable journey ahead.

The Impact of Jim Henson's Legacy

Before embarking on our exploration, it's essential to acknowledge the ongoing resonance of Jim Henson's legacy. His influence continues to shape contemporary entertainment, and this introductory chapter will delve into the reasons behind his enduring impact.

Jim Henson's life was a symphony of innovation and imagination. Throughout the pages of this book, we will navigate the intricate chapters of his life, unearthing pivotal moments, connecting with the people who shaped his journey, and paying homage to the iconic characters and worlds he brought to life. This biography aims to capture the essence of a man whose dreams knew no bounds and whose creative strings still pull at our hearts today.

Chapter 1:
Roots of Imagination

In the quiet town of Greenville, Mississippi, on September 24, 1936, James Maury Henson was born to Paul and Betty Henson. He grew up in a close-knit family alongside his younger siblings, Jane and Paul Jr. His early years were marked by a fascination with the world around him, as he absorbed the stories and creativity that would eventually shape his future.

Henson's first foray into the realm of puppetry occurred during his teenage years. In 1949, at the tender age of 13, he crafted his first puppet, a wooden-headed character named Sam. The birth of this puppet marked the beginning of Henson's lifelong passion for bringing inanimate objects to life.

As Henson continued to hone his artistic skills, he found inspiration in the emerging medium of television. He enrolled at the University of Maryland in 1954, where he pursued a degree in home economics with a focus on visual design. It was during his college years that Henson's creative talents truly began to flourish.

The Henson Family and Early Influences

To understand the man behind the Muppets, one must delve into Henson's family background. His parents, Paul and Betty, fostered an environment of encouragement and support for their children's creative pursuits. Paul Henson worked for the U.S. Department of Agriculture, and Betty Henson, an avid painter, infused their household with artistic expression.

Formative Years: Childhood and Education

Growing up in Hyattsville, Maryland, young Jim Henson demonstrated an affinity for art and storytelling from an early age. He found solace in crafting intricate puppets and hosting puppet shows for friends and family. These early performances served as the seeds of his future artistic endeavors.

The Birth of Puppetry Passion: Henson's First Puppet Experiments

The year 1949 marked a significant turning point for Henson. Intrigued by the potential of puppetry as a means of storytelling, he fashioned his first puppet, Sam, using a coat hanger, felt, and ping-pong balls for eyes. The success of Sam's puppetry debut at a local TV station talent show fueled Henson's determination to explore the endless possibilities of this art form.

Exploration of Theater and Visual Arts

In 1954, Henson's enrollment at the University of Maryland opened doors to formal training in the arts. His studies in home economics exposed him to disciplines ranging from painting and drawing to costume design and puppet fabrication. These skills would prove invaluable as he later embarked on his journey to revolutionize puppetry and entertainment.

As we journey through the formative years of Jim Henson's life, we witness the emergence of his creative spirit and the roots of his future innovations. From his family's nurturing influence to his early puppetry experiments, each moment laid the groundwork for the exceptional artistic legacy that would unfold in the years to come.

Chapter 2:
Crafting Characters

With the backdrop of a burgeoning television industry and a world on the cusp of transformation, Jim Henson's journey into the realm of puppetry continued to gain momentum during the mid-1950s. As he pursued his studies at the University of Maryland, Henson's creative energy was matched only by his determination to carve out a unique niche in the world of entertainment.

Henson's College Years: Exploring Theater and Visual Arts

In 1955, Henson's enrollment at the University of Maryland proved to be a pivotal juncture in his creative development. He immersed himself in the study of theater arts, honing his acting skills and deepening his understanding of visual design. This period marked the convergence of his innate artistic talents and his growing interest in performance art.

The First Puppeteering Successes: "Sam and Friends"

Building on the success of his first puppet, Sam, Henson collaborated with his friend and fellow student, Jane Nebel, to create "Sam and Friends," a five-minute puppet show that aired on WRC-TV in Washington, D.C. The show featured a cast of characters, including

Sam, Yorick, and Harry the Hipster, and introduced viewers to Henson's innovative puppetry techniques.

In 1957, Henson's innovation expanded with the introduction of the Muppet character Kermit, a lizard-like puppet fashioned from Henson's mother's discarded coat and a pair of ping-pong balls for eyes. Kermit quickly became a fan favorite, foreshadowing the iconic status he would later achieve.

Collaborations and Creative Partnerships

During these formative years, Henson's collaborative spirit flourished. He formed partnerships with fellow students, artists, and puppet enthusiasts, forging connections that would shape the trajectory of his career. Notably, his collaboration with Jerry Juhl, a fellow University of Maryland student, marked the beginning of a creative collaboration that would endure for decades.

As the 1950s drew to a close, Henson's reputation as a visionary puppeteer began to spread beyond the local television circuit. His dedication to the art of puppetry, coupled with his pioneering techniques, laid the groundwork for the exceptional journey that lay ahead.

Pioneering Techniques and Artistic Expression

Henson's dedication to innovation was evident not only in the characters he created but also in his commitment to pushing the boundaries of puppetry. He experimented with lip synchronization, allowing his puppets to speak in sync with his own voice. This technique breathed life into his characters, setting them apart from traditional puppetry.

The mid-to-late 1950s marked a period of intense growth and exploration for Jim Henson. From his early successes with "Sam and Friends" to the birth of Kermit the Frog, each endeavor showcased his unwavering dedication to his craft and his ability to transform the art of puppetry into a dynamic and captivating form of entertainment.

Chapter 3: Laying the Foundation

As the 1960s dawned, the world was undergoing profound social and cultural changes, and Jim Henson's creative journey mirrored the evolving landscape. This chapter delves into the pivotal decade that witnessed the birth of the Muppets, Henson's collaboration with groundbreaking educational programs, and the establishment of an enduring legacy that would captivate audiences of all ages.

The Birth of the Muppets: From TV Commercials to "Sesame Street"

The early 1960s marked a period of exploration for Henson as he expanded the reach of his puppetry. He created a series of innovative commercials featuring his Muppet characters, which caught the attention of advertisers and audiences alike. These commercials showcased Henson's ability to inject humor, charm, and personality into inanimate puppets.

In 1969, Henson's vision aligned with the groundbreaking educational goals of the Children's Television Workshop (later known as Sesame Workshop). This collaboration led to the creation of "Sesame Street," a revolutionary children's program that combined entertainment with education. Henson's Muppet characters, including Big Bird, Ernie and Bert, and Cookie Monster, played pivotal roles in delivering lessons through play and imagination.

Kermit the Frog: Iconic Creation and Evolution

Throughout the 1960s, Henson's beloved Muppet characters continued to evolve, none more iconic than Kermit the Frog. Kermit's transformation from a simple lizard puppet to a charismatic frog with a distinctive voice showcased Henson's dedication to character development and innovation. Kermit's gentle demeanor and wit would make him a cultural touchstone for generations to come.

Muppets on the Rise: Expanding Reach and Popularity

By the mid-1960s, the Muppets were capturing the hearts of audiences beyond television commercials. Appearances on variety shows and talk shows introduced the Muppets to a wider audience. Henson's imaginative blend of humor, puppetry, and storytelling resonated with both children and adults, setting the stage for the Muppets' ascension to pop culture stardom.

Innovative Techniques and Collaborations

During this period, Henson continued to refine his puppetry techniques. The use of rods and mechanisms allowed for more intricate and expressive movements in his characters. Collaborations with puppeteer Frank Oz further elevated the Muppets' ability to convey emotions and connect with viewers on a profound level.

The Global Impact of "Sesame Street"

The debut of "Sesame Street" in 1969 marked a watershed moment in Henson's career. The program's innovative approach to education and inclusivity resonated around the world. Henson's Muppets became international ambassadors of learning, diversity, and the power of imagination.

The 1960s witnessed Jim Henson's transformation from a puppeteer experimenting with characters to a visionary creator shaping the landscape of children's programming and entertainment. The birth of the Muppets and the global impact of "Sesame Street" cemented Henson's place in history as an artistic pioneer and advocate for meaningful content for all audiences.

Chapter 4:
Reaching for the Stars

The 1970s marked a period of unprecedented creativity and expansion for Jim Henson. With the successful launch of "The Muppet Show," Henson's puppetry prowess reached new heights, captivating audiences of all ages and solidifying his status as a creative force to be reckoned with. This chapter delves into the golden era of the Muppets, their journey to the silver screen, and the recognition that Henson's groundbreaking work garnered.

The Muppet Show: Concept, Creation, and Launch (1976)

In 1976, Jim Henson's vision for "The Muppet Show" became a reality. The variety show format, blending comedy, music, and guest appearances, provided a perfect canvas for the Muppets to shine. The irreplaceable Kermit the Frog took on the role of the show's charming host, guiding viewers through a whimsical world filled with laughter and camaraderie.

Debuting in September 1976, "The Muppet Show" quickly became a global sensation. The show's unique combination of puppetry, humor, and live performances showcased Henson's knack for creating characters that resonated with audiences of all ages.

Behind the Scenes: Innovative Techniques and Creative Challenges

Behind the laughter and applause of "The Muppet Show" lay a world of innovative puppetry techniques. The skilled puppeteers, led by Henson himself, utilized rods, wires, and animatronics to bring characters to life. The seamless blending of these techniques with human guest stars showcased the magic of Henson's artistry.

As the show gained popularity, creative challenges also arose. Henson's dedication to maintaining high-quality content while balancing the demands of producing a weekly show required constant innovation and collaboration with his team.

Hollywood Calling: Henson's Venture into Films and Awards

The success of "The Muppet Show" propelled Henson into the world of feature films. In 1979, "The Muppet Movie" hit theaters, blending the Muppets' signature humor with a heartwarming narrative. The film's success cemented the Muppets' place on the silver screen and introduced their unique charm to a broader audience.

Recognition for Henson's contributions poured in during this era. Notably, in 1978, he received the Silver Buffalo Award from the Boy Scouts of America for his positive impact on young audiences. Additionally, "The Muppet Show" earned several Emmy Awards, further validating Henson's groundbreaking approach to entertainment.

Continued Innovation and Expanding Influence

Beyond "The Muppet Show" and film endeavors, Henson continued to experiment with his craft. His pioneering work in animatronics led to the creation of life-like creatures that seamlessly interacted with humans, as seen in projects like "The Dark Crystal" (1982).

The 1970s were a period of prolific creativity and recognition for Jim Henson. The laughter of "The Muppet Show," the success of "The Muppet Movie," and the accolades he received showcased Henson's ability to craft worlds of wonder and imagination that transcended generations and united audiences around the globe.

Chapter 5:
Pushing Boundaries

As the 1980s dawned, Jim Henson's creative vision expanded into uncharted territory. This chapter delves into a period of ambitious projects and boundary-pushing endeavors that would cement Henson's reputation as a visionary artist. From the dark depths of "The Dark Crystal" to the lighthearted antics of the Fraggles, Henson's imagination knew no bounds.

"The Dark Crystal" (1982): A Visionary Fantasy

In 1982, Henson embarked on a monumental project that would challenge the conventions of puppetry and storytelling. "The Dark Crystal" was a groundbreaking fantasy film set in a richly detailed world populated entirely by puppets. Henson's collaboration with artist Brian Froud led to the creation of a visually stunning universe, complete with intricate creatures, languages, and lore.

The film's release marked a departure from the Muppets' signature humor, delving into a darker and more mythical narrative. "The Dark Crystal" showcased Henson's dedication to pushing artistic boundaries while remaining committed to storytelling that resonated on an emotional level.

The Fraggle Phenomenon: Building Worlds with Depth

While "The Dark Crystal" explored a new artistic dimension, Henson's creative versatility was also evident in "Fraggle Rock" (1983). This unique television series introduced audiences to the whimsical world of Fraggles, Doozers, and Gorgs. Henson's commitment to creating multi-layered narratives that appealed to both children and adults was evident in the show's themes of friendship, cooperation, and environmental awareness.

Ventures Beyond Puppets: Henson's Expanding Creative Palette

Henson's creative pursuits extended beyond traditional puppetry during this period. He continued to explore the intersection of technology and entertainment, experimenting with computer-generated imagery (CGI) and animatronics. His desire to integrate these elements into his projects showcased his forward-thinking approach to storytelling.

The 1980s also saw the emergence of the Jim Henson Foundation, dedicated to promoting puppetry as a vibrant and innovative art form. Henson's commitment to nurturing emerging puppeteers and fostering creativity underscored his desire to leave a lasting legacy.

Legacy of Innovation and Imagination

As the early 1980s drew to a close, Jim Henson's ventures into uncharted creative realms became emblematic of his fearless pursuit of innovation. "The Dark Crystal" and "Fraggle Rock" illustrated his ability to craft immersive worlds, challenge conventions, and touch the hearts of audiences through imaginative storytelling. Henson's influence on the arts was no longer limited to the realm of puppetry; he had become a pioneer in multiple domains, leaving an indelible mark on the landscape of entertainment.

Chapter 6:
Winds of Change

As the mid-1980s arrived, Jim Henson navigated a period of transition and diversification in his creative pursuits. This chapter explores Henson's expanding horizons, from business endeavors to cinematic innovations, as he continued to redefine the boundaries of his artistic legacy.

Business Ventures: Muppets, Disney, and More

The mid-1980s witnessed a shift in Henson's involvement in the business aspects of his creations. In 1984, Henson Associates, Inc. (later known as The Jim Henson Company) entered into negotiations with The Walt Disney Company for a potential merger. Although the deal eventually fell through, this period marked Henson's exploration of new horizons beyond the creative sphere.

During this time, Henson also formed Jim Henson Productions, focusing on film and television projects beyond the Muppets. This diversification allowed Henson to explore different genres and platforms, showcasing his versatility as a creator.

"Labyrinth" (1986): A Visionary Blend of Fantasy and Puppetry

Henson's cinematic innovations continued with "Labyrinth," a fantasy film released in 1986. Combining live-action performances with puppetry, animatronics, and intricate set designs, the film showcased Henson's ability to seamlessly merge different visual elements into a cohesive narrative.

Collaborating with artist Brian Froud once again, Henson created a world filled with fantastical creatures, intricate landscapes, and a narrative that captivated audiences. The film, while not an immediate commercial success, has since achieved a cult following and stands as a testament to Henson's commitment to pushing the boundaries of cinematic storytelling.

Muppet Babies and Continuing TV Influence

Henson's influence continued to thrive on television screens as well. "Muppet Babies," an animated series that reimagined the Muppet characters as youngsters, debuted in 1984. The show combined animation with puppetry, introducing the Muppets to a new generation of viewers while maintaining Henson's commitment to quality and creativity.

Adventures Beyond Puppets: Innovation and Exploration

As Henson diversified his creative pursuits, he continued to innovate across various mediums. His exploration of emerging technologies, including the use of animatronics and CGI, demonstrated his ongoing commitment to pushing the boundaries of visual storytelling.

In 1987, Henson received the Special Trustees Award at the Emmy Awards for his pioneering work in the field of children's television and puppetry. This recognition underscored his lasting impact on the entertainment industry.

Honoring Jim Henson's Values: Social and Environmental Contributions

Throughout this period, Henson's dedication to social and environmental causes remained unwavering. He was actively involved in various charitable endeavors, including initiatives that supported education, health, and the environment.

As the 1980s drew to a close, Jim Henson's legacy extended beyond puppetry and entertainment. His ventures into new business realms, cinematic innovations, and commitment to values-driven initiatives showcased a multifaceted creator whose influence would continue to shape culture and inspire generations to come.

Chapter 7:
Legacy and
Lasting Impact

The final chapter of Jim Henson's life is a testament to his enduring influence and the indelible mark he left on the world of entertainment. As the 1990s began, Henson's legacy continued to evolve, with his creations taking on new dimensions and his values resonating through various endeavors.

Jim Henson's Creature Shop: Bridging Art and Technology

In the early 1990s, Henson's creative innovations found a home in the establishment of Jim Henson's Creature Shop. This multidisciplinary workshop brought together artists, designers, and technicians to collaborate on projects ranging from film and television to theme parks and advertising.

The Creature Shop furthered Henson's legacy of blending artistry with technology, creating creatures that blended realism and imagination. This period saw the shop's involvement in projects such as "Dinosaurs," "The Flintstones," and "Teenage Mutant Ninja Turtles," showcasing its versatility and impact across various media.

"The Muppet Christmas Carol" and Final Works

In 1992, the Muppets returned to the big screen in "The Muppet Christmas Carol." This adaptation of Charles Dickens' classic tale showcased Henson's enduring characters in a beloved narrative, continuing to bring joy and laughter to audiences.

Henson's final directorial effort, "Muppet Vision 3D," premiered in 1991 at Disney's Hollywood Studios. The attraction combined 3D film technology with live performances and in-theater effects, underscoring Henson's ongoing pursuit of groundbreaking storytelling techniques.

Remembering Jim Henson: His Passing and Commemoration

Tragically, on May 16, 1990, Jim Henson's life was cut short at the age of 53 due to complications from a bacterial infection. His passing sent shockwaves through the entertainment world and beyond, leaving a void that could never truly be filled.

In the wake of his passing, a memorial service was held at the Cathedral of St. John the Divine in New York City. Friends, colleagues, and fans gathered to celebrate Henson's life, contributions, and enduring impact on the arts.

Legacy of Creativity and Values

Jim Henson's influence extended far beyond his lifetime. His legacy lives on through the continued work of The Jim Henson Company, which has remained dedicated to nurturing innovative storytelling and artistic creativity. The Henson family also established The Jim Henson Foundation, which continues to support and promote puppetry as a vibrant and vital art form.

Beyond the entertainment industry, Henson's values of creativity, imagination, and kindness have resonated through generations. His characters, from Kermit the Frog to Big Bird, continue to teach valuable life lessons to young and old alike.

In reflecting on Jim Henson's legacy, it becomes clear that his contributions extend beyond mere entertainment. He was a visionary artist, a trailblazer in puppetry and technology, and a beacon of joy and compassion in an often complex world. His influence endures, reminding us all that the strings of creativity he wove will continue to inspire for generations to come.

Chapter 8:
Posthumous Pursuits

Even after his passing, Jim Henson's impact on the world of entertainment and creativity remained undiminished. This chapter explores the evolution of The Jim Henson Company, the ongoing projects that carry Henson's spirit, and the ways in which his legacy continues to touch hearts and minds.

The Henson Company's Evolution: From Family to Corporate Ownership

Following Jim Henson's death, his son Brian Henson took on an increasingly prominent role in the management of The Jim Henson Company. Brian's dedication to preserving his father's legacy while exploring new creative horizons led to the company's involvement in a wide range of projects, from television and film to digital media and live performances.

In 2000, the German media company EM.TV acquired The Jim Henson Company, signaling a shift towards corporate ownership. However, the Henson family's ongoing commitment to the company's values and creative ethos remained steadfast.

Expanding the Legacy: Projects, Exhibits, and Partnerships

Throughout the years, The Jim Henson Company continued to produce new content while honoring its iconic past. Projects like "Farscape" and "Sid the Science Kid" demonstrated the company's versatility and commitment to innovative storytelling.

Henson's influence extended beyond the screen as well. The Center for Puppetry Arts in Atlanta established a permanent Jim Henson Collection, showcasing puppets, props, and memorabilia from his illustrious career. Additionally, traveling exhibitions and collaborations with museums around the world ensured that Henson's work reached audiences of all ages.

Honoring Jim Henson's Values: Social and Environmental Contributions

The Jim Henson Foundation, established by Henson's family, continued to champion puppetry as an art form. The foundation provided grants to emerging puppeteers, fostering creativity and innovation in the field.

Henson's legacy of giving back extended beyond the arts. The company remained involved in charitable initiatives, supporting causes related to education, healthcare, and environmental conservation. This commitment to social responsibility echoed Henson's lifelong values.

An Enduring Inspiration

As years turned into decades, Jim Henson's influence remained vibrant. His characters, stories, and approach to creativity continued to resonate with audiences around the world. Reboots and adaptations of Henson's classic works introduced new generations to the magic he brought to entertainment.

In 2016, The Jim Henson Company celebrated its 60th anniversary, a testament to the enduring legacy of its founder. Jim Henson's impact on the arts, his dedication to innovation, and his belief in the power of imagination ensure that his legacy remains alive and well.

Conclusion: A Legacy That Lives On

The story of Jim Henson is one of innovation, creativity, and the ability to touch hearts on a global scale. His journey from puppetry experiments to global acclaim showcases the boundless possibilities of imagination. The legacy of Jim Henson is not confined to the pages of history; it lives on in the laughter of children, the wonder of adults, and the creative spirit that continues to be ignited by his timeless creations.

Appendix A: Key Dates and Milestones

This appendix provides a comprehensive timeline of key events and milestones in the life and career of Jim Henson, offering a chronological overview of his remarkable journey from puppetry experiments to global icon.

1936

- September 24: Jim Henson is born in Greenville, Mississippi.

1949

- Creates his first puppet, Sam.

1955

- Enrolls at the University of Maryland, pursuing studies in home economics and visual design.

1957

- Collaborates with Jane Nebel to create "Sam and Friends," a puppet show featuring early Muppet characters.

1960

- Henson's Muppets start appearing in commercials, showcasing his unique approach to puppetry.

1969

- Collaborates with Children's Television Workshop to create "Sesame Street," revolutionizing children's television.

1976

- "The Muppet Show" debuts, becoming a global sensation and introducing beloved characters.

1979

- "The Muppet Movie" is released, marking the Muppets' transition to the silver screen.

1982

- Creates the fantasy film "The Dark Crystal," showcasing groundbreaking puppetry techniques.
- Establishes Jim Henson's Creature Shop, a multidisciplinary workshop for creative projects.

1983

- "Fraggle Rock" premieres, capturing imaginations with its whimsical world and characters.

1984

- "Muppet Babies" introduces a new generation to the Muppet characters.

1986

- Releases "Labyrinth," blending live-action performances with puppetry and animatronics.

1990

- May 16: Jim Henson passes away due to complications from a bacterial infection.

1992

- "The Muppet Christmas Carol" is released, continuing the legacy of Muppet films.

1991

- "Muppet Vision 3D" debuts, combining 3D film technology with live performances.

2000

- The Jim Henson Company is acquired by the German media company EM.TV.

Present

- The Jim Henson Company remains active in various creative projects, continuing to honor Henson's legacy.

Conclusion

The key dates and milestones outlined in this timeline offer a glimpse into the extraordinary life and contributions of Jim Henson. His journey from humble beginnings to global acclaim is marked by innovative achievements that continue to inspire and captivate audiences around the world.

Appendix B: People and Collaborators

This appendix highlights the individuals who played pivotal roles in Jim Henson's creative journey, from his earliest experiments with puppetry to his groundbreaking accomplishments in the world of entertainment.

Jane Nebel

- Collaborator and co-creator of "Sam and Friends," Henson's first puppet show.
- Partner in the early development of Muppet characters and techniques.

Jerry Juhl

- Collaborator and writer who worked closely with Henson on various projects, including "The Muppet Show" and "Fraggle Rock."
- Contributed to the unique humor and heart of Henson's creations.

Frank Oz

- Collaborator and puppeteer who brought life to iconic characters such as Miss Piggy and Fozzie Bear.

- Co-directed "The Dark Crystal" with Henson and continued to collaborate on subsequent projects.

Brian Henson

- Jim Henson's son who continued his father's legacy as a puppeteer, director, and producer.
- Led The Jim Henson Company into new creative directions following Jim Henson's passing.

Brian Froud

- Artist and illustrator known for his collaborations with Jim Henson on projects like "The Dark Crystal" and "Labyrinth."
- Played a pivotal role in shaping the visual aesthetics of these iconic films.

Caroll Spinney

- Puppeteer behind the beloved characters Big Bird and Oscar the Grouch on "Sesame Street."
- Collaborated with Henson on numerous occasions, contributing to the enduring impact of the Muppets.

Richard Hunt

- Puppeteer who brought characters like Scooter, Janice, and Beaker to life on "The Muppet Show."
- Collaborated closely with Henson in the development of new characters and performances.

Dave Goelz

- Puppeteer behind iconic characters such as Gonzo, Bunsen Honeydew, and Boober Fraggle.

- Played a key role in the technical innovation and characterization of the Muppets.

Conclusion

The individuals listed in this appendix are just a few of the many people who contributed to the magic and creativity of Jim Henson's world. Their collaborations and contributions enriched Henson's projects with unique talents, insights, and dedication, ultimately shaping the cultural phenomenon that continues to captivate audiences to this day.

Appendix C: Comprehensive Works List

This appendix provides an extensive list of Jim Henson's major works, spanning from his earliest puppetry experiments to his groundbreaking achievements in television, film, and beyond. The list serves as a testament to Henson's prolific creativity and enduring impact on the world of entertainment.

Television:

- "Sam and Friends" (1955-1961)
- "Sesame Street" (1969-present)
- "The Muppet Show" (1976-1981)
- "Fraggle Rock" (1983-1987)
- "Muppet Babies" (1984-1991)
- "The Jim Henson Hour" (1989)
- "The Storyteller" (1987-1989)
- "Jim Henson's Mother Goose Stories" (1990)
- "Dinosaurs" (1991-1994)
- "Secret Life of Toys" (1994)

Film:

- "The Muppet Movie" (1979)
- "The Great Muppet Caper" (1981)
- "The Dark Crystal" (1982)

- "The Muppets Take Manhattan" (1984)
- "Labyrinth" (1986)
- "The Muppet Christmas Carol" (1992)
- "Muppet Treasure Island" (1996)
- "Muppets from Space" (1999)

Specials and Shorts:

- "Emmet Otter's Jug-Band Christmas" (1977)
- "The Christmas Toy" (1986)
- "The Tale of the Bunny Picnic" (1986)
- "Jim Henson's Muppet Video" series (1985-1987)
- "Jim Henson's Little Muppet Monsters" (1985)

Innovative Projects:

- "Jim Henson's Creature Shop" (Established in 1982)
- "Muppet Vision 3D" (1991)

Legacy and Continuation:

- The Jim Henson Company (Founded in 1958)
- The Jim Henson Foundation (Established in 1982)

Honors and Recognitions:

- Recipient of multiple Emmy Awards for puppetry and contributions to children's television.
- Silver Buffalo Award from the Boy Scouts of America for positive impact on young audiences.

Conclusion

The comprehensive works list presented in this appendix showcases the breadth and depth of Jim Henson's creative endeavors. From pioneering puppetry techniques to crafting beloved characters and narratives, Henson's legacy is an enduring testament to the power of imagination and storytelling.

Made in the USA
Las Vegas, NV
24 March 2025

20067166R00042